I0441678

Neuro Linguistic Programming

A Practical Guide To Taking Charge Of Your Life By Changing Your Brain And Mind

Michelle Janson

Disclaimer

The information presented in this book is for the purposes of entertainment and education only. In downloading and reading this book, the reader agrees to hold the author harmless concerning any outcomes sustained as the direct or indirect result of implementing or attempted implementation of the ideas and concepts contained herein. If you have, or suspect you have, any medical condition you are strongly advised to seek the help of a suitably-qualified professional as soon as possible. This book is in no way intended as a substitute for such advice or services.

Contents

Introduction – What Is Neuro Linguistic Programming?

Congratulations on choosing to download and read this book! In doing so, you are taking huge steps forward in your personal development. You are about to learn the basics of an approach that can change your life if you apply the principles and techniques on a regular basis. NLP was developed over 40 years ago, and practitioners have been using it ever since to help people conquer a range of problems in a safe, effective manner.

We will begin with an overview of Neuro Linguistic Programming (NLP) – its history, what it can do, who can learn it, and what it can do. In subsequent chapters, you will learn about the underlying assumptions behind NLP before picking up some techniques you can learn and begin implementing today. Finally, you will read about the many ways you can apply NLP across all areas of your life, from work to parenting to romantic relationships. Get ready to learn a set of skills that will enable you to change your life!

What exactly is NLP?

Let's start by breaking the term down into three separate parts:

Neuro: This refers to properties of the brain, specifically its abilities to think, plan and imagine. The brain is a highly plastic organ, meaning that it has the potential to change in response to stimuli. The implications of this are exciting – it means, as NLP practitioners will tell you, that provided we take care to feed our brains with the right stimuli, they will respond positively.

Linguistic: The word 'linguistic' means 'relating to language.' A major component of NLP is the words and phrases we use to communicate to ourselves and others. NLP practitioners recognize that the ways in which we talk have a major impact on the way we perceive ourselves and the world in which we live.

Programming: When you install a programme on a computer, you are improving its capabilities and expanding its range of functions. In a similar fashion, NLP is about altering the way your mind and brain work in such a way that makes you more adaptable and better-able to function even in challenging situations. In NLP speak, programming refers to the experiences we have that shape our thoughts and ultimately our behaviours.

In sum, NLP is an approach that takes a careful look at the messages we send to ourselves and others – both verbal and non-verbal – and how these messages can influence our thoughts, mood states and behaviours. As you can imagine, this can have an enormously influential effect on our mood states and the way we choose to live life.

A key figure in NLP defines it in this way:

"...a model of interpersonal communication chiefly concerned with the relationship between successful patterns of behavior and the subjective experiences (esp. patterns of thought) underlying them...a system of alternative therapy based on this which seeks to educate people in self-awareness and effective communication, and to change their patterns of mental and emotional behavior."

- Dr Richard Bandler, co-founder of NLP (via NLPTraining.com)

Where did NLP come from?

In the 1970s, a University of California, Santa Cruz student by the name of Richard Bandler began to work with one of his professors, John Grinder, to develop a new form of psychotherapy that would combine existing theories and methods of high-profile, successful psychotherapists such as Fritz Perls (the founder of Gestalt Therapy) with applied linguistical analysis.

Over the years, the original founding group took NLP in various directions as various disagreements and splits occurred. The story of the various factions within NLP is too lengthy for a book of this size, but for you as a practitioner the historical background is not too important. For further technical details on the founding theory of NLP, the following books may be of interest: The Structure Of Magic Volumes I and II (1975, 1976), Changing With Families (1976), and Patterns Of The Hypnotic Techniques Of Milton H. Erickson Volumes I and II (1975, 1977).

Since its inception in the 1970s, NLP has been adopted by a

number of trainers, coaches and psychologists across numerous contexts including business, education, and one-to-one psychotherapy. NLP is not a trademarked term, and today describes a broad collection of practices and approaches to personal change. The theory and techniques you will learn in this book cover the basic, most commonly-held beliefs held by NLP practitioners and some common NLP methods for inducing positive life change.

What are the key benefits of NLP?

NLP requires that you take a close look at your existing patterns of behaviour and ways of thinking that are holding you back, or keeping you stuck in negative mood states. It provides a formalised, step-by-step way of pulling apart your current worldview and exchanging behaviours and beliefs for more constructive ways of approaching life.

Here are just some of the positive side-effects of practicing NLP:

Improved motivation: NLP exercises help – amongst other things – you in imagining a better, more exciting future in which you meet your goals and enjoy a higher quality of life on a day-to-day basis. When you start to imagine an alternative future for yourself, change becomes a reality and this in turn motivates you to keep moving forward. This doesn't mean that every day will be perfect, but it does mean that you are more likely to get out of bed in the morning ready to face the day and embrace the challenges it brings.

Eliminating bad habits: Do you suffer from bad habits such as smoking, overeating or difficulties controlling your temper? Do you tend to talk to yourself in a negative way, procrastinate, or drink too much? NLP can help you overcome these issues and more. By altering how we see the world, our own capabilities and the potential for change, we increase our power over bad habits and replace them with a healthier way of relating to ourselves, others, and the world around us.

Increased self-control/control over your emotional state: NLP practitioners emphasise that we can change our moods and control strong emotions by altering the way we talk and think about the situation at hand. Imagine how much happier and more productive you will be when you learn how to deal with a low mood or the resurfacing of an unhappy memory! Too often, we become distracted by the negative thoughts in our heads, or waste hours wallowing in toxic mood states. Once you learn how to loosen the hold that emotions have over you, you can look forward to a more productive and relaxed life.

Improved mood: If you struggle to hold onto good feelings and often seem to be at the mercy of your emotions, learning to control how you respond to external events can be enormously empowering. Once you have learned to master your emotions and feel secure in the knowledge that a bad mood need never get you down for long, this will make you a happier person in general. In turn, you will feel more positively about the world and about life, making you more inclined to take part in activities and reach for a career and hobbies that increase this satisfaction. NLP won't turn you into a permanently happy person – nothing can do that! – but it can certainly help improve your overall enjoyment of life.

Increased tolerance of other people: NLP practitioners emphasise that people make the best decision possible based on the information they have available to them at the time (more on this in the next chapter). This means that they – just like you – are doing the best they can. When you internalise this, you begin to be more tolerant of others, even when they make mistakes or act in ways you may be tempted to dismiss as stupid. Not only will increasing your tolerance make you a nicer person who is better-able to make friends, but it will also cut down on your stress levels. How much time do you currently waste judging other people? Wouldn't it be nice to reclaim that time and energy and put it to a more positive use?

Better communication skills: NLP places great emphasis on building rapport with other people, and using this connection as the basis for productive communication. Improving your communication skills will help you better collaborate with other people, and also improve your chances in getting your needs met. This in turn will improve your life satisfaction. On a more practical level, the communication skills taught in NLP can be of special benefit to people in certain careers. For example, if you are salesperson, knowing how to strike up a rapport with a customer can be crucial in closing a deal.

Improved relationships: The bedrock for all successful

relationships is solid communication. Many relationships – whether romantic, platonic, business, or other kinds – suffer because one or more parties fail to communicate their needs and expectations in an appropriate manner. NLP will help you identify your own needs and those of other people, and give you the tools to address them in a mature and responsible way.

NLP can also help you when it comes to choosing suitable friends and romantic partners. When you have a strongly-developed sense of self, you become more inclined to be choosy about the people with whom you spend your time. This results in a virtuous cycle: You value yourself and think positively, so you choose people who mirror similar values and live in a healthy way, which in turn promotes your self-image as a person with worth and a great life, which attracts healthy people to you, and so on. NLP is also useful in the aftermath of a relationship breakup, helping you to reframe and process painful memories and feelings. This sets you up to learn from what went wrong in previous relationships so you can make better choices next time around. No longer will you make the same mistakes over and over again!

Improved employment prospects: If you work for someone else, NLP will improve your work performance and subsequently increase your opportunities for job advancement and overall work satisfaction. Employer's value workers who take a positive attitude, can communicate well with others, and who are self-confident whilst remaining humble enough to take feedback and advice. NLP will also help you to become more flexible in your behaviour, another asset that will make you highly desirable to any employer. If you are self-employed, NLP will be invaluable in helping you remain focused, kick procrastination and self-doubt, and grow your vision of the business you are looking to develop. Communicating with clients and partners will also become easier when you implement NLP, and this can only be good news for your turnover!

Improved ability to take on challenges: When you feel as though you have greater control over your own life, a positive self-image and the knowledge that you can handle whatever life throws at you, you feel more inclined to take risks. When you realize that with the right approach, no emotion or event need have a huge amount of power over you, this liberates you to take new risks. Whereas previously you may have feared failure or ridicule from others, thus forcing you to remain in your comfort zone, NLP can help you realise that life is there for living and even the most unpleasant or difficult of emotions can be handled successfully.

Improved self-esteem: When you make a commitment to improve your life, this has positive knock-on effects for your self-esteem. Demonstrating to yourself that change really is possible and that you have the power to become who you want to be sends a signal to your subconscious mind that you matter, that you are taking yourself seriously, and that there is hope for the future. Combined, these can all add up to a significant self-esteem boost. You will start to take a more proactive approach to your life in general, and begin to reach your full potential.

Achieve your goals: NLP teaches you how to become more self-aware, to visualize a better future, and to start working towards making that vision a reality. This makes you more likely to achieve your goals, which will enhance your mood and overall life satisfaction. NLP exercises can help you along the road to your targets even when obstacles threaten to get in your way or your mood dips.

Who can practice NLP?

Anyone who is capable of understanding the basic principles and theory behind NLP and can concentrate for several minutes at a time can use it to improve their lives. Even young children can be taught how to visualise positive outcomes and talk to themselves in a constructive rather than negative manner (further instructions on these kinds of exercises are contained later on in the book). NLP can be used as an add-on treatment for people with existing mental health problems, provided they are under the supervision of a suitably-qualified therapist.

NLP is particularly suitable for people who are facing specific challenges or want to improve particular aspects of their lives. For instance, it can be used to increase self-confidence, to overcome a particular fear or phobia, or to kick a bad habit once and for all.

Are there any risks associated with NLP?

NLP is a pain free, drug-free, low-cost way of creating personal change. The worst that can happen is that nothing happens at all!

There is no way to damage yourself by implementing the methods you will learn in this book.

However, NLP is not a substitute for any medical care you may already be receiving. If you have a mental health problem, always consult with your doctor, therapist or other suitably-licensed professional before implementing these ideas. If you are working with a therapist, they may be keen to help you make the best possible use of ideas from NLP.

If you would like more help in making the techniques outlined in this volume work for you, you could seek out an NLP-trained therapist with which to work. If you are in the UK, visit the website of the Association For NLP (anlp.org) and click the 'Find A Professional' link under the 'Resources' tab on the homepage. If you are in the USA, visit the American Union of NLP (aunlp.org) and click the 'Practitioners' link. Please remember, however, that NLP is not trademarked and anyone is entitled to call themselves an NLP expert or NLP therapist. Always take the time to ask your practitioner about their experiences, training and professional background. Anyone worthy of your time and money should be happy to tell you why they are trustworthy. Remember too that there is no law that says you must stick with the first therapist you find – if you don't feel a rapport with someone, try another therapist. Your personal development is worth the time and effort.

The Key Assumptions of NLP

This chapter will introduce you to the general assumptions shared by those who practice NLP. They are not methods in and of themselves. Rather, they present an important framework for you to refer to as you begin your path as an NLP practitioner.

You may be wondering at this point why we are not moving straight to step-by-step instructions that will allow you to implement NLP techniques. However, there are two good reasons why it's important to cover a bit of theory before jumping to the practical tips. Firstly, the assumptions themselves can change your life. That's right – even if you read no further than to the end of this chapter, learning about the mindset behind NLP as a discipline can be enough to change your view on life for the better!

Secondly, understanding the theory allows you to to gain a full appreciation of the techniques we will cover later in the book. This means you will be more motivated to implement NLP into your daily life and therefore increases the chances that it will exert a meaningful effect.

Some of these assumptions may seem very alienating at first, yet it is essential that you internalise them if you are to fully embrace everything that NLP has to offer. Read through each one slowly, and think about how your life could change if you altered your mindset.

You may initially feel that some of these assumptions are wrong or unlikely. If this happens, ask yourself two questions:

1. Can I suspend my judgment long enough to test out this assumption and see whether it has a discernibly positive impact on my life?

2. How well are my current beliefs serving me? What have I got to lose by swapping my current belief system for these new assumptions?

Assumption 1: Rather than asking whether a belief is 'right,' we should ask whether it is useful.

This is the primary assumption that underlies all the others in this list. If you are naturally of a sceptical bent – and there's nothing wrong with that! – you might be inclined to ask for evidence that the following assumptions are 'correct.' However, NLP practitioners don't spend much time worrying whether or not they can be proven right. For them, the key question is whether adopting a particular outlook on life is helpful or not to the person concerned.

For instance, if you look further on in this chapter, you will see that Assumption 3 is stated as follows: 'Everyone is capable of change.' You may be tempted to respond to such an assertion with an anecdote of your uncle/friend/next-door neighbour who, you are quite certain, could never change. You might wonder where the proof is – can it really be said that everyone can alter their approach to life?

NLP practitioners would praise your critical thinking abilities, but gently ask you to consider whether the validity of such assumptions is really the most pressing concern here. When it comes to your personal wellbeing and personal ability to make changes, is it helpful to take the assumption as true? In all probability, yes, such a stance will help you. If you believe that everyone is capable of change, then this includes you. Isn't that a great foundation for making a real difference in your own life? You are much more likely to give NLP – and indeed, anything else you set your mind to – a better try if you adopt the belief that we are all capable of change.

Assumption 2: One of the most important determinants of a person's happiness and success is the degree to which they can adapt to new circumstances and challenges.

Although we all vary in the extent to which we embrace and cope with change, as a species we tend to cling on to what is safe and familiar. This can be seen from a very young age – babies and young children will tend to stick close by their parents, especially in new or dangerous situations.

As we get older, we learn that the world is often an unpredictable place with many potentially dangerous situations of which we need to remain aware. Of course it is healthy to be slightly wary of the unknown – this natural wariness is one reason why the human race has lasted as long as it has! – but at the same time, too much fear or an over-cautious personality can hamper personal growth. If you are reluctant to embrace or even consider taking a positive attitude to change, you will be forever struggling in life. Why? Because, as they say, the one constant in life is change. It takes just a few seconds for a life to be forever altered. Everyone faces numerous challenges in life, everyone grows older, and everyone has to cope with the fact that nothing stays the same for very long.

If you can accept that change is natural, normal and inevitable, your grip on life will loosen and you will begin to feel more relaxed. Although you will realize that nothing good can last forever, this also applies to the bad stuff! That is, although you may rightly realize that good relationships, jobs, etc. often come with a sell-by date, on the other side of the equation you can take much comfort in the realisation that negative feelings and unpleasant situations don't last forever either.

NLP practitioners believe that one of the most positive, empowering things anyone can do is learn to thrive in the face of change. This means being able to control your feelings and behaviours when change does occur, and readily identify when you need to change a particular way of thinking or feeling about a particular subject. When you have the abiity to manage change – and even to enjoy it – you become a popular employee, colleague and relationship partner. People like those who remain calm when everything is up in the air.

Assumption 3: Everyone is capable of change.

Even if you believe yourself to be a creature of habit, you are capable of dramatic change. Although some of us appear to be more flexible than others, everyone is born with a brain that is capable of being re-molded and rewired via experience. The actions you take and the words you use have a discernible impact on the way you think.

Just think about the changes you have undertaken so far in your life. Even if you would say that your life until now has been relatively unexciting, you have still already proven that you can learn new skills and adapt to new settings. For a start, consider the sheer number of new skills you have had to learn as an infant. You had to learn to speak, walk and relate to other people. Then you had to go to school, which required you to adapt again to a whole new environment. Then you went to high school, possibly followed by college, then a job, then possibly another job, parenthood, meeting your partner – and on and on. Unless you were born in a cave and literally lived there all your life, you have all the evidence you need that you are capable of change. With the NLP tools outlined later in this book, you can expect to succeed in making any change you want.

Here's a final thought. If you are still uncertain as to whether you are capable of making the changes you want to make, remind yourself that you went so far as to download a book on NLP and read past the first few pages. Even if your conscious mind seems reluctant to loosen its grip on your previous way of life, at some level you crave change. Keep reading!

Assumption 4: Our representation of reality/the world should not be mistaken for reality itself.

We don't react to the world as it really is – we react to the map of the world we have in our heads. You may have heard a saying that goes something like this – 'The map is not the territory.' This means that we carry with us an idea of how the world is (and how the world 'should be'), but that this does not necessarily correspond with either the most realistic or most positive view open to us.

To put it another way – our life experiences are profoundly affected by the attitude we take to the world around us, and how we choose to interpret our life experiences. Two people could live in exactly the same kind of house in the same town and have the same amount of income available, yet hold two very different views of the same situation. Person A bemoans the fact that their house is too small, that there is little to do in the town, and that they wished they earned more money. Person B, however, is happy to live in a small house that requires very few hours to clean each week, little money to maintain, and is unlikely to be a target for burglars. They may also realise that they live in a small town, but focus on the sense of community rather than wish that there were more attractions to visit.

Who is 'right'? It's hard, if not impossible, to say. NLP practitioners maintain that there are many ways of viewing the world, and there is no method we can use to ascertain which is the 'best' way of looking at a situation. However, what we can do is think about the most helpful way of looking at the world. In applying this criteria, the person with the positive attitude towards their town and living situation is in the better position.

Again, it is about choosing to be happy rather than right.

Assumption 5: Everyone makes the best possible decision based on the information and skills they have available to them at the time.

When you internalize this assumption, you will be less inclined to pass judgements, both on yourself and on others. At its root, this assumption is about assuming that when we make a choice as to how to behave, we are doing so based on the resources we have available at the time. This can make a huge difference in how you perceive yourself and others.

NLP practitioners help themselves make better decisions by expanding their resources and skills. For instance, prior to practicing NLP, you may not have had the skills or motivation to quit smoking. Therefore, when it came to making a decision – should you or should you not have that cigarette? – given your lack of resources, you could only make one decision, and that decision is to give into your cravings and smoke.

Assumption 6: It is impossible to avoid communicating, both to yourself and those around you.

Every moment you spend awake is a moment in which you are sending out messages, both to yourself and those around you. Obviously, we experience ourselves as communicating when we speak to someone else – we want them to understand our message and respond appropriately.

However, there are other forms of communication that demand our attention. NLP trainers often say that you can't NOT communicate! Even if you choose to remain silent and sit quietly in a corner of a busy room, this is still a form of communication – you are telling everyone, without saying a word, that you really do not want to be there. Body language is extremely hard to control.

Another facet of communication that most people forget – possibly because they take their internal communication system for granted – is the messages they send themselves. For instance, many people who become anxious and depressed on a regular basis typically talk to themselves in an unkind and overly-critical way. This rarely motivates them to change. In fact, criticism often has a depressing effect that shuts down motivation. NLP exercises challenge us to take a close look at the messages we send ourselves, and how negative thought patterns can be exchanged for those of a more positive nature.

Assumption 7: What you focus on becomes your reality.

Have you ever heard the saying, 'Focus on what you want, not what you don't have?' A key assumption in NLP is that visualisation is a powerful tool, and we render a particular outcome more or less likely by focusing upon it. This can be done in a positive way, for instance by athletes who visualize winning a race before they run it. NLP practitioners, as you will learn later on, do something similar with various life situations.

However, visualisation can also be used negatively and keep you stuck in old patterns of behaviour and to keep you focusing on what you lack. For instance, if you find yourself struggling with social anxiety, you may find that your mind conjures up unhelpful but compelling images of nerve-wracking, awkward moments just prior to a party or other event. This teaches your mind and body that social situations are to be feared, which reinforces the very behaviours and feelings that you want to be rid of! This is where NLP comes in – it can help you exchange your negative images and expectations for positive visualisation.

Assumption 8: There is a strong, intimate connection between the mind and the body.

The western world is increasingly coming to appreciate that the mind and body are closely linked. If you think back over your own experiences, you will probably agree that this makes sense on an intuitive level. For instance, many people feel literally sick with nerves before an important job interview or a first date with someone they like. When someone you love dies or leaves you, it is common to feel a sense of heaviness or pain in your chest, which some people describe as a broken-hearted feeling.

This assumption is used in NLP exercises as the basis for interventions that rely on making certain physical movements to induce positive mood states. For instance, the 'calm anchor' technique uses a sense of pressure (elicited by drawing the thumb and forefinger of one hand together and squeezing firmly) coupled with positive feelings learned by association. This is covered in greater detail later in the book.

Assumption 9: There is no real 'failure,' only feedback.

Successful people know that behind every triumph often lies a history of failed projects and attempts at innovation that never lead anywhere. They realise that overnight success without hard work is largely a myth. They also learn from their mistakes and carry these lessons forward so that their next attempt is more likely to be a success. They see 'failure' as a sign to do something else, not to give up entirely. They remember the Dalai Lama's teaching – 'sometimes not getting what you want is an enormous stroke of luck.'

Take a moment to imagine how different your life could be if you spent less time feeling bad about things that didn't go to plan, and instead learned what you could take from the situation? Wouldn't you be more inclined to take risks, which in turn would take you closer to your goals?

NLP practitioners do not just use this idea as a general guiding idea in their lives, but they also apply this principle when using specific NLP exercises. For instance, if a particular visualisation or anchor (which you will learn about in detail over the coming pages) does not work, they simply learn from the experience and better tailor the process to the individual.

Now you have an understanding of the principles underlying NLP, it's time to get started with some practical tips and exercises you can use to enhance your mental health and psychological wellbeing today! Turn the page and let's get started.

Practical NLP Techniques You Can Use Today

In this chapter, you will learn the following techniques. They will help you regulate your emotions, influence others, and improve your chances of success in all areas of your life.

1. Reframing

2. Grounding

3. Confidence Visualization

4. Anchoring

5. Whiteout

6. Negative Belief Blaster

7. Dissociation

8. Creating Rapport

9. Compulsion Killer

10. Silencing   The   Inner   Critic

Exercise 1: Reframing

This technique will help you change your feelings towards a particular event. This will further your ability to handle even difficult situations, and in turn will boost your confidence. Your intention here isn't to adopt an unconditionally positive view of a situation – that would be an unrealistic goal, and in any event it isn't practical to deliberately overlook negative aspects of our lives just because we wish things were different! However, we can choose to take a more positive attitude to almost any event without losing our grip on reality. Reframing helps you do just that. This lessens the hold that particular memories have over you and leaves you free to pursue a more positive future. When you know that you are able to cope with bad memories, it means you are more likely to

To begin with, pick a memory or problem that persistently leaves you feeling unhappy whenever you think of it. For instance, let's imagine you have recently lost your job and are in the process of looking for new employment. Looking for a job can be hard work, and some days you might find yourself dwelling on the fact that you were fired, that you feel bad, and that life is tough. This kind of thought will not inspire you to move forward. You need to find a way of reconceptualising it so as to minimise its psychological impact.

To reframe a memory, start by calling it to mind. Mentally imagine the scene. Blow it up bigger and bigger, until you 'feel' as though you were there all over again. Notice how you feel. In the example mentioned above, you might feel angry and powerless.

Now consciously reframe the situation. Imagine taking a couple of steps back from the mental image. Shrink it a little in your mind's eye. Consider how you could view the situation in a positive way. For instance, leaving your job allows you the opportunity to find a new position and shake up your life for the better. Really make an effort to think about the same situation but from a new angle. Encourage this new emotion – hope, excitement, or even relief if you hated your old job – to overwhelm you. Focus on these feelings as you look again at the memory in your mind's eye. Repeat this exercise until your primary response to the memory in question is positive rather than   negative.

Exercise 2: Grounding

This is an excellent basic exercise that sets the stage for many other NLP practices. In grounding yourself, you are immediately exerting a calming effect on your body and mind. This will make you more receptive to NLP exercises, increasing the chances of rapid and lasting change. It can also be used as a simple, effective means of inducing a relaxed state whenever and wherever you like. If you are having a stressful morning at work, for example, shut the office door for a few minutes and get ready to feel better quickly.

Begin by removing your shoes and socks. Stand with your feet flat on the ground. If possible, do this exercise outdoors to make it extra relaxing! Take deep breaths in and out. Stand with your arms held loosely by your sides, with your feet approximately shoulder width apart. Close your eyes. Now imagine yourself anchored to the ground in such a way that nothing can unbalance or disturb you.

Wriggle your toes slightly and imagine that they are holding onto the ground beneath you, holding you steady. Keep your legs straight, but avoid locking your knees. Inhale, then as you release the breath make a conscious effort to drop your shoulders slightly. Imagine, as you exhale, your feelings of tension and worry leaving your body.

Once you are in a relaxed state, shift your attention to your lower abdomen, 2-3 inches below your belly button. Make yourself aware of the tension in those muscles, and how they hold you upright. Realise how grounded you now feel. Open your eyes and keep your gaze soft and steady. Tell yourself how relaxed you are and how you can cope with anything life throws at you. Keep your breathing deep and even.

Practice this exercise for a few minutes every day, and you will begin to feel naturally more grounded without trying. Be sure to re-direct your attention to that point below your navel every so often. This way, you are teaching yourself to feel calm, relaxed and unruffled whenever you shift your focus to that part of your body.

After a few days, try maintaining this state of relaxation and groundedness as you walk around. With practice, you will be able to induce a highly relaxed, confident state whenever you need it. This technique is invaluable in high-pressure situations such as job interviews or having a high-stakes conversation with someone you respect and admire.

Exercise 3: Confidence Visualization

What separates confident people from those with low self-esteem and relatively lower levels of belief in their own capabilities? One important factor is their ability to imagine more favourable outcomes. Remember, a key assumption in NLP is that the mind exerts a powerful effect on the body, and vice versa. When you envisage a certain mental or physical state for yourself, the more likely it is that you will be able to access and sustain it.

Close your eyes and imagine that you have suddenly been cloned. Take a minute to imagine this carbon copy of you, so that its existence feels as real as you can possibly make it. Now picture your identical twin standing or sitting opposite you. Begin by imagining them to be exactly the same as you.

The next step is to gradually mould them into a confident individual who knows that they can achieve whatever they want to get from life. For example, you could imagine your clone to have better posture, a louder and smoother speaking voice, and a confident smile. Take your time to imagine these details. Make the transformation as vivid as possible. Notice how this cloned, altered version of you moves and talks. What is their energy or 'vibe' like? How would other people know that they are a confident person?

Once you have built a steady image of this new version of yourself, imagine stepping forward and into the body of this clone. You should automatically feel yourself beginning to adopt their posture and way of speaking. Smile and take a deep breath in, imagining as you do so that you are absorbing all the very best qualities of this other 'you.'

Exercise 4: Anchoring

When you create an anchor, you condition yourself to associate a physical movement or gesture with a feeling of your choice. Once you have formed this connection, you have a way to readily access this particular feeling whenever you wish. The power of this technique should be obvious. Imagine being able to head off feelings of hurt, disappointment and general annoyance simply through the use of a hand movement?

To create your anchor, you need to begin by feeling the relevant state. For instance, let's say you want to create a 'happy' anchor – a movement or gesture that allows you to feel content whenever you want. Your first step is to access feelings of happiness. Close your eyes and locate a happy memory. Pick a time in which you felt truly content and glad to be alive. Picture yourself in that moment, paying attention to every little detail – how you looked, what you were wearing, the expression on your face, and so on.

As you imagine the scene, make sure that your body language is also congruent with the state you are trying to evoke. For instance, when creating a happiness anchor, you would ensure that you were smiling during this step.

Once you have accessed this emotion, it's time to create a physical anchor. Press your thumb and forefinger together firmly as you focus on your mental image. Keep imagining and pressing for around a minute. Open your eyes and take a few deep breaths, before repeating the exercise from the beginning. Do this exercise every day for a week and you will create a link between the anchoring act of squeezing your thumb and forefinger together with the feeling of being happy. The next time you are in a bad mood or difficult situation, simply use your anchor to change the way you feel.

You can create as many anchors as you need and want for various positive feelings, but remember to use a new physical motion or sensation for each, otherwise the connections will become muddled! For example, you could use a happiness anchor as described above, and also create a 'calm' anchor using your feet – you could create a link between feelings of relaxation and the sensation of pressing your toe firmly down against the sole of your shoe. Anything that is easy to remember and discreet will work well.

Exercise 5: Whiteout

If you find yourself thinking the same old troublesome memories time and time again, or suffer from intrusive thinking, using a whiteout technique can bring you great relief. Whiting out a mental image lessens the emotional effect it has on you, and with regular practice you will soon find that it will lose its power to impact on you at all.

Close your eyes and bring to mind a mental image that causes you trouble. It may be an embarrassing memory or a painful scene from your past. It could even be something that hasn't actually happened, but still represents a source of torment – you may be plagued by a particular fear around public speaking, perhaps imagining yourself forgetting your words or blushing uncontrollably. Whatever the image, bring it to mind and concentrate on it.

The next step should be done rapidly and decisively. Imagine seeing the image in full color, but then turning up the brightness so much that it is literally whited out. If you have ever experimented with the brightness settings on a digital camera or in image manipulation software, you could use this as a 'model' for what such a whiteout would look like.

Take a deep breath and distract yourself by thinking of something neutral and totally unrelated to the mental image with which you are working. Then repeat the steps outlined above, taking a few moments between each 'round' of whiting out to think of another topic. This gives your brain a chance to solidify the connection between the mental image and the act of whiting it out.

Do this enough times and after a while, you will struggle to remember the original image at all. Even if you do, the effect is has on you will likely be greatly diminished. You can do this for as many memories or other kinds of images as you like.

Exercise 6: Negative Belief Blaster

Negative self-talk is a significant barrier that many of us face when trying to make positive changes in our lives. If you carry around voices in your head that tell you that you 'can't' do X, Y or Z then your chances of progressing and making headway towards your goals will be greatly diminished. Remember that NLP practitioners place a strong emphasis on whether our thoughts are useful or not, and the majority of our persistent negative thoughts are of very little use whatsoever! Fortunately, you can use this exercise to eliminate them.

Firstly, think of belief that you know to be false. For instance, you might choose to think about your unbelief that grass is pink. As you dwell on this belief, notice the image it conjures up in your mind's eye. Hold that image firmly in your mind. Now imagine that the image is whited out, as in the Whiteout exercise described earlier in this section. Alternatively, you could imagine the image being screwed up and thrown away like an unwanted flyer. Do this several times until it is easy for you to envisage getting rid of a faulty and unwanted belief in this way.

Now think about an unhelpful, negative belief you hold about yourself, your life or the world in general. For instance, you may think 'I'll always be alone and single,' and see a mental image of yourself as a lonely cat lady (or gentleman) flash up in your mind's eye. Adopting the same approach as you took with the previous trivial example, either white it out or give it the 'screw it up and throw it away' treatment. Practice this a few times until it feels natural to discard your unhelpful belief in this way. Work through each negative belief you hold about yourself, one at a time. If you are like many people, you will have quite a lot of material to get through! This is fine – schedule a few minutes each day for your NLP practice and within a couple of weeks you will start to notice significant changes with regards to how you talk to, and about, yourself. Other people will start to notice that you are becoming a more positive person in general.

Exercise 7: Dissociation

Do you ever wish that you could somehow step back from your most distressing or destructive thoughts, or somehow take a break from your own mind? This dissociation exercise can help you do just that. It provides you with a quick sense of emotional relief, allowing you to take on the role of an objective observer. This helps you not only react in a more constructive way to emotive situations, but also helps you in keeping your temper when others annoy you. Therefore, this exercise can be helpful in improving your relationships. It is especially good for recurring fears and phobias.

To see how this technique works, let's imagine that your working life is more difficult than it ought to be because you become nervous whenever you see your boss, who is frequently in the office. Because they make you nervous your productivity is impaired, and so you decide to use this technique to lessen these negative feelings.

Firstly, conjure up a mental image or 'mental movie' of the scene. The important aspect of this step is to imagine yourself not from your own perspective, but as an impartial third party who has just happened to come into the room and watch the scenario unfold. To continue with the example stated above, you would imagine watching yourself working at your desk, seeing your boss come in through the door and starting to show signs of anxiety such as foot-tapping, sweating, and shuffling papers around. You would imagine watching yourself greet your boss in an anxious tone of voice.

Once you have imagined the scene as an objective observer, it's now time to manipulate the movie! Firstly, play it backwards. That's right – do a mental re-wind. If you have ever rewound a DVD or video you will know that this typically looks quite comical, and so when you apply a similar effect to your mental movie your emotional response should start to dampen immediately. Do this a couple of times – watch the 'movie' in your mind's eye, then rewind.

The next step is to mentally add some light-hearted music to the film. Watch the film being re-wound as the amusing music plays. Do this two or three times. By this point, the emotional response previously triggered by the memory or fear should have changed significantly. If not, simply repeat the above steps a few more times until you have well and truly loosened your old associations between that particular mental image and certain unwanted feelings.

Exercise 8: Creating Rapport

NLP isn't just applicable to the messages you send to yourself. It's also about creating and sustaining better-quality relationships with other people. If you stop and think about it, human relationships make the world go round. Whether it's smoothing over interactions with your family, increasing the strength of your friendships or closing an important business deal, it's useful to have the skills required to 'tap into' other peoples' thoughts and feelings.

A good way to appear more approachable, friendly and empathic is to learn to build rapport with other people. NLP practitioners use a few techniques to facilitate this. Firstly, they stress the importance of body language. Have you ever noticed that the way you hold yourself has a huge impact upon the way you feel? It's difficult to sustain a happy, upbeat mood if you sit with your shoulders slumped, for example. Now think about how other peoples' body language makes you feel. If you've ever arrived at home or at the office feeling upbeat and glad to be alive only to be confronted by a sullen relative or co-worker who clearly communicating dissatisfaction via their body language, you will be all too familiar with the power that other peoples' posture and facial expression can have!

Fortunately, you can also use this piece of psychology for the power of good. When you next want to develop a sense of closeness and understanding with someone else, subtly match their body language. Humans naturally feel more comfortable with those who appear to understand us and share in our thoughts and opinions. We may not consciously realise it, but when someone else's body language mirrors our own, we feel reassured.

However, you need to be careful when mirroring so as not to appear too obvious! Do not immediately copy every single thing your conversation partner is doing. Rather, mimic only a few gestures, and allow a few seconds to elapse before shifting your own limbs or changing your facial expression.

A more advanced technique is known as 'pacing.' To pace someone is to make them follow your lead without them even realising what you are trying to do. An experienced NLP practitioner is able to use his or her body language skills to build rapport and then influence the other party into thinking, feeling or behaving a certain way.

For example, let's say that your colleague is having a bad day at work, and their negativity is draining you. You want them to feel more excited about the project your team is working on, and to lift their mood. To pace them, you could start by holding a conversation in which you match their body language – you may speak quietly, move slowly, and adopt a slightly slumped posture, to echo what they are currently feeling. However, after a few minutes, you could begin to adopt more positive movements and change your voice to a more energetic, upbeat tone. You would pay attention to the way in which your co-worker responds to you. If you are skilled at pacing, you would notice that they would gradually start to mirror your positive body language, and because the mind follows where the body leads, they would begin to feel more cheerful. By the end of the conversation – and the entire interaction need last no longer than 20-30 minutes to elicit such a result – you would both be feeling good!

Finally, another useful NLP technique in building rapport is to share in your partner's submodalities. A submodality is simply a way of communicating and interpreting information via the senses – we can communicate via touch, taste, hearing, and so on. If you can tune in to the submodality favoured by another person, you can adjust your own communication accordingly. They will then feel as though you understand them more readily.

The best way to access someone's preferred submodality is to listen carefully to their choice of words. For instance, suppose you are talking to a client in an attempt to negotiate a deal, and you want to build a rapport with them. Listening to them speak, you may pick up phrases that indicate they are in a visual or 'seeing' submodality – 'I can picture it,' they might say, or 'I'm seeing a particular vision of….,' and so on. This is valuable information, because it allows you to mirror their preferred verbal communication in much the same way as their body language. You can then weave visual-based words and phrases into the conversation, perhaps saying things like 'If we consider the bigger picture…' or 'Our company has the foresight to meet your future needs.' This is a subtle but effective way of building rapport. The other party will feel as though you are on their wavelength, and will be more likely to trust and respect you as a result.

Exercise 9: Compulsion Killer

Do you struggle with bad habits, such as smoking, drinking or biting your fingernails? Wouldn't it be great to have a quick and simple exercise on hand to help you overcome your urges to engage in compulsive behaviour? Try this NLP exercise to help kill your cravings!

Begin by bringing to mind the thing or behaviour you crave, or have trouble resisting. For instance, let's say that you want to get out of the habit of eating so much chocolate. In this exercise, you would therefore bring to mind an image of your favourite chocolate bar.

Now take a minute to examine this mental image in your mind's eye. Take note of the properties of this image. How large is it? How colourful is it? Do you experience it as being close to you, or quite far away? Is this image in sharp focus? Does it have a border? Don't overthink the answers to these questions, just go with your gut instinct. Note them down.

The next step is to bring to mind a neutral image. For instance, let's say that whilst you struggle not to eat chocolate, cigarettes leave you utterly indifferent, so you conjure up a mental image of a cigarette for this part of the exercise. Again, note the following properties of this mental image: its size, its colour, and its position in space, and the other factors listed in the paragraph above. You will probably find that your compulsive and non-compulsive images differ along these dimensions.

Now that you have made the comparison between the compulsive and non-compulsive images, your task is to mentally experiment with the relevant variables until your compulsive image loosens its hold on you. For instance, you may have noticed that the size of the mental image associated with the chocolate bar (your compulsive image) is much larger and more vivid than the mental image associated with the cigarette (your non-compulsive image). In order to lessen the compulsion, you can turn up the size and vivid colour until it is mentally overwhelming and completely unappealing. Every time you experience the compulsive image, you would mentally blow it up and make it so intensely colourful that it loses all meaning and becomes quite ridiculous. Repeat this several times and you should find that you no longer find your previously compulsive images quite so compelling.

Exercise 10: Silencing The Inner Critic

Many of us find that our productivity dips and moods suffer due to our Inner Critic. Most of us have one – it's that annoying voice in your head that feeds you unhelpful and negative information. The Inner Critic frequently tells you that you 'can't' do certain things, or that something is bound to go wrong, and that you shouldn't even bother trying to improve your situation.

Of course, thinking only the best of every situation and person isn't a healthy approach either – a realistic attitude to life is necessary if we are to avoid taking stupid risks or getting our hopes up! But in general, the Inner Critic is not helpful and if we can quieten it, life will typically become more satisfying.

The next time you hear that nagging voice in your head, try this exercise. First, pay attention to the tone of your Inner Critic's voice. Is it your own voice, or that of someone else? Once you have listened to it for a few seconds, imagine applying a sound filter or special effect, and make it sound silly and squeaky. How authoritative does this voice sound now?

Now consider where, exactly, the voice is coming from. In all likelihood, you will experience it as coming from the back of your head. But what if you imagined it coming from your little toe, or your ankle? Doesn't the Inner Critic seem suddenly a little less credible? In fact, once you have imagined your ankle feeding you pointlessly negative sentiments, that inner voice will seem almost laughable! It's amazing what a little creative visualisation can do.

NLP in Work, Parenting and Relationships

When you begin applying the philosophy and techniques outlined in this book, you will see substantial shifts occur in all areas of your life. To give you further motivation and ideas, this section will briefly outline how NLP can help you with work, parenting and relationships.

NLP at Work

When you learn to silence your inner critic, you will become more motivated to take risks which in turn will allow you more opportunities to succeed. Using the confidence visualisation technique will improve your performance in situations in which communicating a sense of self-belief is vital, such as in making presentations to clients or senior management. Reframing is also tremendously valuable in your professional life, as it allows you to take negative feedback or situations you would previously have regarded as failures and encourages you to learn from them for the future. This begins a virtuous cycle – you learn to make progress based on feedback, which means that you are likely to behave differently (and to succeed!) next time, which will bring with it further (more positive) feedback, and so on.

NLP and Parenting

You can use NLP techniques in two ways to improve your parenting experience. Firstly, you can use the techniques described in this guide to increase rapport, which will deepen the relationship between you and your children. You can use pacing to gently persuade sullen teenagers into seeing your point of view, which is a much more pleasant approach compared with shouting matches and arguments!

You can also teach some of these techniques to your children directly. For instance, if you have a child who suffers from low confidence, the Negative Belief Buster is an easily-learned way of boosting their self-esteem. If your son or daughter has problems with anxiety, the Anchoring technique is a safe, easy-to-use way of helping them feel calm wherever they are.

NLP and Relationships

In applying what you have learned in this guide, your relationships will improve. Here are just a couple of examples of the ways in which this might happen. Let's say that you have been arguing with your partner more often than is usual lately – perhaps you have both been under a lot of strain at work, and as a result keep bickering over relatively minor issues such as whose turn it is to take the garbage out. Employing the Dissociation technique, in which you take on the role of a third party, would be an excellent way of diffusing the situation.

Another useful technique for those in troubled relationships is the Whiteout. If you find yourself ruminating on old grievances or unpleasant memories – say your partner had an affair a long time ago, but the associated mental images keep on returning and they cause you distress – learning to quickly white them out can allow you to move on with your life and focus on how your relationship is right now, in the present. Using such techniques allows you to move on from grudges and petty grievances.

If you are single, know that NLP can help you in your quest to become a more attractive partner. For instance, confident and secure people are generally considered to be more attractive. When you learn to become more confident and to silence your Inner Critic, this will show through in your day-to-day behaviour. If you find that you tend to attract needy or negative people, you will be delighted to discover that when you become more positive yourself, the calibre of mates you draw in will be much higher. Give it a go and see the results!

Conclusion

Thank you for reading this introduction to NLP! You now have at your disposal tools to help you better succeed in every area of your life. Make NLP a consistent part of your daily routine and look forward to increased confidence and efficiency. Remember that change takes time, so give yourself a few days or even weeks to notice the significant changes that can and will occur! If you have enjoyed and benefitted from this book, hope you share with your friends and people you care. Thanks!

www.ingramcontent.com/pod-product-compliance
Lightning Source LLC
Chambersburg PA
CBHW060645290526
45793CB00001B/410